DECORATING WITH
DECOUPAGE

To Francesco

ACKNOWLEGEMENTS

Many people have helped me write this manual, whether directly or indirectly.
I would like to give heartfelt thanks to everyone, particularly to my family and my father,
for their participation and useful tips.
To my husband, Andrea, for his patience and the photographs presented in the chapter
"Doors and Windows".
To Antonella, for her role as a proofreader.
To Luisa and Piera of the Paper Factory for their presence and advice.
And to all the friends who encouraged and motivated me while I was writing this manual.

My special thanks go to the companies which kindly offered their materials and objects:
MAIMERI – Bettolino di Mediglia (Milan), for the colors, tools, and subsidiary products.
CARTERIA TASSOTTI – Bassano del Grappa (Vicenza), for the numerous decorated papers
and prints.
"LE SCATOLE" – Milan, and in particular to Signora Giovanna for the boxes, both plain and
decorated.
DIAT of Enrico Dell'Acqua & C. Milan, for all the wooden objects.
Warm thanks to Alberto Bertoldi for his photographs, and the time spent together.

Library of Congress-in-Publication Data Available

10   9   8   7   6   5   4   3   2   1

Published in 2001 by Sterling Publishing Co., Inc.
387 Park Avenue South
New York, NY 10016

First published in Italy by RCS Libri S.p.A
under the title *Decorare con il découpage*

©1999 RCS Libri S.p.A, Milan
©2001 English translation by Sterling Publishing Co., Inc.

Distributed in Canada by Sterling Publishing
c/o Canadian Manda Group, One Atlantic Avenue, Suite 105
Toronto, Ontario, Canada M6K 3E7
Distributed in Great Britain and Europe by Cassell PLC
Wellington House, 125 Strand, London WC2R 0BB, England
Distributed in Australia by Capricorn Link (Australia) Pty Ltd.
P.O. Box 704, Windsor, NSW 2756, Australia

Every effort has been made to ensure that all the information in this book is accurate.
However, due to differing conditions, tools, and individual skills, the publisher cannot be
responsible for any injuries, losses, and other damages which may result from the use of
the information in this book.

Sterling ISBN 0-8069-6969-5

Francesca Besso
DECORATING WITH
DECOUPAGE

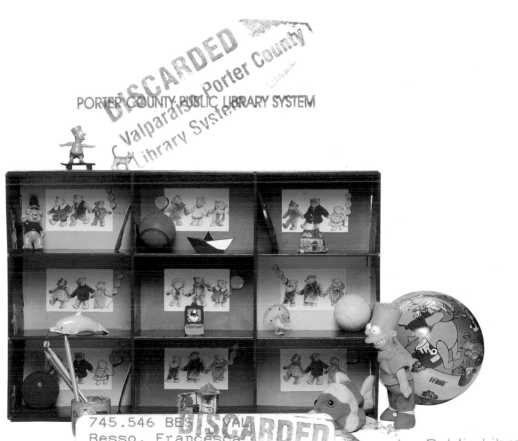

Sterling Publishing Co., Inc.
New York

CONTENTS

INTRODUCTION

Decoupage is often defined as an amateurish technique for decorating various kinds of surfaces, but its possibilities are so vast that the interpretative flair, imagination, and taste of the creating person can turn it today, as in the past, into a fully-fledged art form.

The choice of the object to decorate, of the paper or fabric to be cut out and glued, and of the possible finishing touches to apply later is so wide that it supplies us with a valid excuse for pleasantly scouring around markets, shops, and even our attics. With decoupage we can decorate all sorts of materials such as terracotta, wood, cardboard, metal (not coated with enamel), glass, porcelain, walls, and many rigid surfaces in our homes. Changing styles, tastes, and fads bring about constant evolutions in our modes of observing and living, and they often stimulate research and experimentation to rediscover ancient techniques to apply to our present-day lifestyles.

The aim of this book, besides that of teaching the basic technique, is to supply more in-depth information regarding the preparation of

backgrounds and the use of finishing touches so that you can create many different effects. They can be used individually, adjoined, or even mixed to highlight your decoration.

Furthermore, tradition requires that various coats of transparent varnish (up to twenty) be applied to the glued cutouts so that the surface has an even thickness. Be in no hurry, therefore, to create a masterpiece in one sitting, as there is the risk of making something banal. It is much better to carefully look around and, if possible, prepare a project beforehand.

Some of the procedures shown, though fairly easy, need only a little patience and some extra effort in order to achieve the original, satisfactory results that you are certainly capable of obtaining.

A BRIEF HISTORY OF THIS CRAFT

Decoupage (from the French verb *découper*, meaning "to cut") dates back to the 12th and 13th centuries. Tiny strips of decorated paper were cut out and glued, just as they were, to small objects or to decorate the edges of manuscripts. It became widespread in 17th century Venice, where it was used to imitate Chinese and Japanese lacquers. In view of the high costs and the restricted number of these imported objects, skillful Venetian furniture makers and craftsmen decided to imitate them by cutting out or copying original Oriental prints, gluing them on their own furniture, and protecting them with a material similar to lacquer. In the 18th century, this technique rapidly spread throughout France, where it was also known as scriban (from "the art of the desk"). People in high society (including Marie Antoinette herself) dabbled in it.

Almost at the same time, the English, who already decorated the walls of their rooms with landscape prints, friezes, and portraits, began to publish books with Chinese and Japanese illustrations to cut out. It was not until the Victorian Age that decoupage caught on as a hobby. Books with romantic floral patterns, picture cards, and even fabrics soon became available. The beauty of the objects decorated with this technique depends greatly not only on the choice of illustrations and their combination but also on the skill and patience with which they are cut out.

The introduction of precut figures from America, Germany, and England in the 19th century and the consequent loss of quality in the decorations led to the gradual decline of decoupage. During the past, few years, due perhaps to a wish to indulge in a pleasant, relaxing craft or maybe thanks to its versatility, decoupage has regained its place as a widely practiced hobby and a highly appreciated craft for creating interior decorations.

An early 18th-century Venetian bureau is shown above. Inner and outer lacquered decorations applied with small, colored print cutouts can be seen.

MATERIALS

PAPERS AND FABRICS

There is such a vast range of papers and fabrics to choose from that one often ends up just falling back on classic materials or those traditionally used for decoupage. Though the latter can be very effective and never lose their charm, do not be afraid of choosing something more modern. To guide you in your choice, we have identified three particular groups: backgrounds, subjects, and borders.

By *backgrounds*, we mean those papers or fabrics devoid of subject (marble, abstract, smudged, or dotted for example) that act as a base for the glued cutouts.

Subjects, on the other hand, are reproductions of flowers, fruits, animals, landscapes, dolls, and geometrical or abstract shapes defined by outlines.

Borders include Greek frets, friezes, etc. which can be used to "frame" the subjects or to enhance the shape of the objects to be decorated. Besides the papers specifically designed for decoupage, you can use paper for pasteboard work, gift-wrapping paper, prints, postcards, colored or black-and-white photocopies, magazine cutouts, and labels. Remember that matte papers are generally more absorbent and are therefore easier to glue (even on large surfaces). Glossy papers are thinner and tend to wrinkle and bubble. It is advisable to remove the back part of postcards prior to use to avoid the cutouts, being too thick. To do this, lift a corner of the postcard with the sharp blade of a craft knife and roll it around a pencil. Proceed slowly to remove the rest. Do not use plastic papers (as they do not absorb glue) or wallpaper if you need to cover corners because they are somewhat rigid and create depth. With regards to magazine cutouts, verify that once dampened they do not show the print from behind. Fabrics, ribbons, lace, cords, and trimmings can be used like paper as long as they are not starched or made with plastic. If they are starched, wash thoroughly in warm water and rinse well.

TOOLS

Most of the tools photographed here, such as scissors, sandpaper, cotton cloths, plastic plates, and cups, are common household objects. For certain projects it may be necessary to obtain several different types of sponge and sandpaper for your tool kit. I recommend that you purchase very soft paintbrushes (synthetic ones will do). They must always be cleaned very thoroughly and used only for your decoupage (paintbrushes containing remnants of varnish or mineral spirits can create difficult-to-remove grease stains). It is also recommended that you purchase a simple plywood board to use as your worktop, a sharp craft knife for the more complex cutouts, and universal white glue (PVA).

COLORS

As the decoupage technique may be applied to almost any type of surface, the range of colors that you can use are just as numerous: watercolors, temperas, enamels, and oils. For practical purposes, I recommend you use water-based acrylic colors; they can be used to create various effects like watercolored, shaded, brush stroked, and relief. They can be mixed together or combined with other composites such as chalk, stucco, glue, and other vehicles (oils, waxes, water, resins, solvent solutions, etc.). If properly diluted, they can also be used as pigments for wood to obtain pastel hues or other particular shades of color. Acrylic colors are ideal as a base on all porous surfaces such as wood, terracotta, cardboard, and rough plastic. On glossier surfaces, it is advisable to mix them with a little bit of white glue. Besides their use for backgrounds, metallic colors such as gold, silver, copper, and bronze are employed for the final touches and to create an antique patina finish.

Pigments are coloring substances in powder form and are essential for the preparation of all colors. They can easily be found in paint and craft shops. When diluted in water, they mix with wallpaper paste, chalk, and all types of water-based paint. If, instead, they are diluted in a few drops of a drying agent and 30% linseed oil or turpentine, they can substitute for oil-based paints. For conveniences sake, I advise purchasing some tubes of burnt umber and sienna artist's oil paint. They will help highlight the cracks and give your work an antique look.

Acrylic chalk is used both for isolating materials which are either too absorbent or for eliminating any defects before applying the colors. When spread with dense brush strokes, it can give pleasant relief effects.

Water or alcohol-based aniline dyes are coloring agents used for wood. They are available in many shades, from light to antique walnut from cherry to mahogany.

Oil pencils when stroked over with a paintbrush soaked in turpentine will create a very soft and luminous effect.

Colored pencils are also very useful for filling in details and giving the finishing touches to your work; use a soft black pencil for the project and a white one for tracing over dark surfaces.

WAXES AND VARNISHES

Just a few simple items are needed to prepare backgrounds: a paint stripper in gel form, if possible ecological and odorless; rubber gloves for protecting your hands; a spatula for removing old paint; fine and coarse-grained sandpaper; steel wool; some cotton cloths; and some poor quality flat brushes with synthetic bristles (they tend to get ruined at this stage). If you are decorating metal objects, obtain rust-resistant paint or red oxide and appropriate stucco. Finishing touches will depend, as you will see later, on personal taste and on the use for which the object is intended. There are endless possibilities available on the market that could turn out to be very costly or not suitable to your work. This is why I recommend you start with some basic products: varnish (glossy, satin, or matte); odorless turpentine or turpentine oil, wax with corresponding solvents (they are more economic and easier to spread); white and raw umber pigments to mix with the wax; final water-based varnish; final fixative spray sealer (for protecting the project); several contrasting hues of aniline dye; and a tube of raw umber oil colors (earth pigments). If you would like to create the crackled effect, purchase specific products (aging varnish and crackling varnish)—they are usually sold in kits. Aging varnish may also be used on its own to create an amber-colored finish. Crackling varnish (water-based) must be added to the aging varnish or to an oil varnish because the chemical reaction between the two is what creates the cracks.

If your object is to be used at home, make sure you always use an nontoxic final varnish.

RELIEF EFFECTS

Old combs, toothbrushes, plastic forks, synthetic or natural sea sponges, and hard flat brushes (even damaged ones) are easily found and can be used to obtain very interesting relief effects. To these, add a couple of handy spatulas and sandpaper. The materials needed to create relatively low-relief effects are: multi-use stucco, white glue (PVA), wallpaper paste (appropriately mixed), and acrylic chalk, which can also be used on its own.

For more accentuated or defined relief work, there are many composites which are easy to use, such as fine *acrylic pumice* (acrylic resin containing crushed pumice), *volume* (acrylic resin in low-density water emulsion), and *acrylic paste for modeling* (acrylic resin containing marble powder).

Metallic acrylics and oil colors brushed over relief contours will also accentuate your effects.

BASIC
TECHNIQUES

CUTTING

A clean, precise contour of the subject is essential in obtaining a good cutout. There are simple shapes, which can be cut out with a pair of scissors, as well as complex shapes, which require the use of a craft knife. Always use the craft knife with the greatest care. With simple shapes, hold the cutout between two fingers and rotate it clockwise while you cut counterclockwise. Remember that your wrist must not be rigid, but should follow the movement of the scissors. With fragile, complex shapes or when the shape has internal parts that need to be removed, it is advisable first to draw small bridges at the thinnest points using a contrasting color. Then proceed slowly as described below, working on a stiff board kept firm and steady.

– Trace small bridges in the thinnest parts of the pattern with a colored pencil.

– With a sharp craft knife, start cutting from inside and then outward. While you follow the contours with the craft knife, turn the paper, as you find most convenient, in such a way that no snips or rigid cuts appear along the curves.

– Hold the pattern
between two fingers and
cut the outside with
a pair of manicure
scissors. Also turn the
page continually to
avoid tearing the
paper at the difficult
points.

APPLYNG THE CUTOUTS

Once the decoration has been cut out, it must be glued onto the support. Have some newspaper or wrapping paper constantly at hand to avoid dirtying your worktop and the back of the cutouts. It is also extremely important to wash your hands very often. If you do not have running water handy, I recommend you keep a basin full of warm water near you while you work in which to rinse your fingers and a clean cloth with which to dry them.

To glue the cutouts onto the support, use standard white glue (PVA) diluted in water in the proportions 5 parts of glue to 1 of water. When using thin or glossy paper or stiff fabrics, dilute the glue in more water to prevent cracks and bubbles from forming. Place the cutout wrong-side-up on some newspaper and spread the glue with a soft paintbrush, starting from the center. Make sure to spread it well on all of the outlines. Do not spread any glue on the bridges, if you have drawn any, so that you can cut them out with a craft knife and remove them after gluing. Should your support be untreated, you can glue the bridges and then paint them with the same color as the background at a later stage.

Proceed following the sequence indicated on the adjoining page. Spread glue at the end on the dry cutout and on the whole surface of the support; it will act as an isolator for the finishing varnishes which, often being oil-based, would otherwise leave indelible stains and haloes on the paper. Then proceed with the finishing touches.

– Spread the glue on the back of the cutout with a soft paintbrush, starting from the center and proceeding outward.

– Apply the cutout to the chosen support, pressing lightly with your fingers from the center and then outward so as to expel any air bubbles.

– Glue down the corners that are still raised, placing a little glue on the back with a flat brush.

– Press a foam-rubber roller (brayer) from the inside and then outward to make the cutout adhere well. After about an hour, apply glue once more over the cutout and over the entire surface of the support.

USEFUL TIPS

We sometimes happen to mentally associate an object with a type of paper that we particularly like. We enthusiastically get down to work only to discover too late that we have made the wrong choice. Of course it is only human to make a wrong guess at times, and not all subjects can have the same beauty, but a short reflection before beginning your work can help you.

Carefully study the object to be covered with decoupage; consider the material, the shape, its intended use, and its style and epoch.

Choose papers that you think are most suitable. Place them one at a time against the object to be decorated and see what looks best in the end. Cut out a detail and place it over the surface, securing it with double-sided adhesive tape. This will give you a rough idea of the result. If the cutout is complex, prepare a project.

To give you a practical example, the boxes shown here seem the same but one is covered in rice paper and vegetable fiber while the other is made of untreated wood. I decided to cover the former with natural warm-toned recycled papers and to use children's patterns. The wood of the latter could be treated with aniline dyes to highlight the grain; I used classical patterns for this one.

THE PROJECT

If the decoration you have chosen is complex (i.e. must be symmetrical, requires a geometrical layout, or overlaps various cutouts), it is best to prepare a project. This is a simple procedure and allows you to work faster. It also helps you to avoid uncertainty when you find yourself holding glued cutouts between your fingers and not knowing where to place them. The project can then be reused or kept in your various work files. Thus, get some drawing or tracing paper, a marker, double-sided adhesive tape, masking tape, and proceed as follows:

– Trace the outlines of the cutouts onto tracing paper.

– Place the tracing paper on the object, following the contours, and secure it on one side with masking tape. Begin gluing on the cutouts, starting with the one underneath, and make sure its position coincides with that of the tracing.

– *Spread a layer of glue over the entire surface of the object and finish it off as preferred.*

PAINT STRIPPING

Removing paint and preparing backgrounds are boring operations, but they are essential if the objects you have decided to decorate are old or if the surfaces, either treated or untreated, are in a bad state. As if that were not enough, the work involved is dirty and the odor of the paint stripper is not particularly attractive. This being the case, I advise working in open-aired spaces (outdoors being the best place). Get yourself a pair of rubber or latex gloves; a brush; a paint stripper (if possible ecological) suitable both for wood and metal; fine- and coarse-grained steel wool; fine and coarse-grained sandpaper; a spatula; and multipurpose filler. Metals require a specific metal proofer and at least two coats of an antirust primer, applied as instructed on the label. If the surface of the wooden object is uneven, it must be filled (with wood filler, synthetic chalk, or any other kind of pore filler) before being painted with the background color. Do not forget that an imperfection or a trace of paint on the surface can add a certain charm to your object, giving it a real antique look.

– With a soft brush spread the paint stripper generously over the surface. Wait until the product begins to react by creating bubbles on the paint.

– Remove the paint with a spatula and, if necessary, apply another coat of paint stripper.

– Rub a damp cloth over the stripped surface. Leave to dry and rub over once more with coarse-grained steel wool.

PREPARING BACKGROUNDS

– Finish off with fine-grained steel wool.

– Fill any imperfections with a spatula and leave to dry.

– Sand with coarse-grained paper.

– Sand with fine-grained paper.

– If the surface is even, you can brush on the aniline dye of your favorite color.

– If the surface is uneven, spread on one or two layers of acrylic chalk. Proceed using the backgrounds you prefer.

SPONGING

This is a quick and easy technique that produces very effective backgrounds. Different kinds of sponges can be used. Natural and synthetic sponges are particularly suitable. The important things to remember are to never overburden them with color and to try them out on a sheet of paper before tackling your object. Templates can be used to create tone-on-tone effects.

– Cut out a round template from an acetate sheet and position it on the support with double-sided adhesive tape. Prepare the acrylic color and begin dabbing, rotating the sponge often.

– Remove the acetate template and dab with a lighter color.

Shown on the opposite page are some of the effects achieved with the various sponges. The first one, a natural sponge, was used for this particular project.

– Add a little bit of white to the last color and dab again. Continue to add color until you obtain the desired effect.

– Glue on the cutouts. When all is dry, cover the entire piece of work with a coat of glue.

SMUDGED BACKGROUNDS

This technique is good for decorating large surfaces such as a tabletop or the doors of a piece of furniture. It is not, however, suitable for walls. If carried out with certain colors it gives a marble effect. The use of a water-based enamel spread over a dry acrylic background will allow you more time for dabbing. Do not forget to rotate the cloth often to avoid producing a stencil effect. Keep a number of cloths handy, as they must always be clean. For a more defined effect, plastic bags may also be used. This technique allows you to work both in negative and in positive. In the first case, proceed by tapping a cloth soaked in water-based enamel on the dry acrylic background. In the second, remove the water-based enamel spread on the dry acrylic background by tapping with a clean pad. The two effects may be combined to create beautiful contrasts; however, it is better to work on a small area of the surface at a time to prevent the enamel from drying.

– Spread two coats of an acrylic color and leave to dry. Prepare the appropriate amount of water-based enamel in a contrasting color and brush it in all directions on a small area. Dab at once with a clean cloth.

– Repeat this operation with a darker enamel over the entire surface. Make sure that you maintain a constant circular motion. Leave to dry.

On the top of the opposite page are, in positive and in negative, the effect obtained by dabbing with a plastic bag. Below, also in positive and in negative, is the effect obtained with a cotton cloth.

– Glue on the cutouts. When they are dry, cover the entire support with glue. If you apply a final glossy water-based varnish, the effect will be enhanced.

OIL PENCILS

Oil pencils can be used on backgrounds treated with chalk or watercolors and on backgrounds treated with enamel or oil. They can be used just as they are, creating graining and nuances of color, or they can be diluted with turpentine until they look just like real oil paintings. Thus, those who are not familiar with canvases and palettes can manage to create works of good quality. Obviously some practice of this technique is necessary, together with a little bit of patience, to obtain attractive brushstrokes.

If you wish to create something quickly, this technique is not recommended; backgrounds made in this way require rather long drying times. Regardless, it is advisable to use good-quality brushes.

– Prepare the background by smudging various shades of the same color together.

– Dip a soft brush in turpentine (making sure not to wet it too much) and pass it rapidly over the surface without pressing.
Leave to dry.

On the opposite page are the effects produced by different types of brushwork. For the first, proceed as per the steps shown. For the second, make a thick crisscross pattern with the oil pencils. Then make "commas" with a small spatula, drawing the color from the top downward. For the third, spread the pencils as before. Then, with a round-headed brush dipped in turpentine, make short brush strokes pushing the color downward.

– Glue on the cutouts. When they are dry, cover the entire surface with glue. Finish off with neutral wax; it will give your work a soft, luminous look.

PAINT WITH GLUE

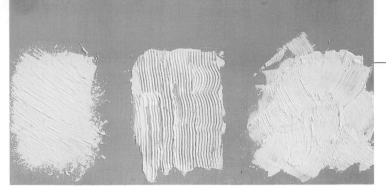

With this technique, which is particularly suitable for surfaces of a certain size, the result is a rather rustic one and recalls folk art creations. Years ago, non-precious woods were hidden by covering the surfaces with chalk or stucco that was then decorated with simple designs. Today, by using synthetic stucco and white glue (PVA) mixed with wall paint, we can imitate those effects while adding more resistance. Prepare the paste with 2 parts of wall paint, 2 parts of multi-use stucco, and 1 part white glue (PVA). Mix well with a spatula. Experiment with soft brushes, toothbrushes, and sponges to see the different results they create. Apply the chosen color with a small dry, flat brush dipped in a little bit of the undiluted acrylic color. Highlight only the parts in relief. Pass lightly over the surface, keeping the brush flat and not pointed. If you wish to give a basic color to the background, add some pigment or acrylic color to the paste, and emphasize the relief with metallic colors such as gold and copper.

– When the paste is ready, spread it generously with uneven brush strokes. Leave to dry.

– Dip a small dry, flat brush in a little bit of the undiluted color. Pass lightly over the surface, holding the brush parallel to the worktop and not pointed. Repeat various times to obtain more color on the background. Leave to dry.

On the opposite page are some of
the effects that can be obtained.
A hard-bristled brush was used on the
first picture, a toothbrush for the second,
and a natural sponge for the third.

– Glue on the cutouts and cover them
with glue.

– When the glue is dry, take the flat brush
and proceed as before, but use a contrasting
color and smudge the outlines of the cutout.
Cover the entire work with glue and finish
with an opaque water-based finishing touch.

ANILINE DYES

Aniline dyes are transparent dyes for wood that can be diluted with either water or alcohol. Water-diluted dyes dry more slowly and may be a little less resistant to light. Alcohol-diluted dyes are more suitable for imitating inlaid work as they dry quicker. Be careful because they are highly flammable once mixed. Therefore, I advise those diluted in water for use in domestic areas. Both dyes, either in powder or already diluted, can be easily found on the market in various colors. They have high coloring properties and I advise spreading them on wood, using more than one diluted coat, until the desired shade is reached. On new, untreated wood, it is best to apply a coat of wood sealer first. With old, puttied wood, it is best to apply a layer of diluted acrylic color because it covers better and also hides any defects there may be. You can create difficult-to-find pastel shades using this technique. Wood is a very absorbent material and aniline dyes tend to spread out on the surface. When dealing with a mock inlay, you must isolate the various areas to be colored with a craft knife, following the outlines traced with a pencil or marker.

– Pass the wood sealer over the raw wood and leave to dry. Then give a light coat of the aniline-dye mixture.

– Trace your design with a fine-tipped felt pen.

– Deeply score the outlines of the design with a craft knife.

On the top of the opposite page is an idea for a children's room that was made with diluted acrylic colors. On the right are examples of shades available on the market, ranging from cherry to mahogany, dark to light walnut, and teak brown.

– Prepare a darker aniline dye and, using a fine brush, color the inside of the design. Leave to dry.

– Glue on the cutouts. When they are dry, cover the entire surface with glue.
Finish off with wax or a transparent varnish.

TROMPE-L'OEIL EFFECT

This technique may seem the most complex, but it actually does not require any special materials—only some cardboard and drawing paper. The secret is to give depth to the cutouts by using mock shading or different perspectives. Have a look at some art books for suggestions, or, if you prefer, there are very simple, clear manuals that can help. At any rate, do not overdo it with heavy shading and forced perspectives; just follow a few simple rules. Remember that shadows are always transparent and are therefore the same tone as the background onto which they are projected. A simple, central perspective outlined by a frame is enough to create a fine sense of depth.

If, however, you are more ambitious and wish to decorate a wall with decoupage using this effect, prepare a precise project to scale.

– Cut out a border and glue it to a piece of cardboard.

– Trace the shadow of the frame (in this case at the inside) with a pencil. Position the cutout and secure it with double-sided adhesive tape. Reproduce the outline with a pencil.

– Remove the cutout and fill in the shadow with a brush, using a very diluted acrylic. On the frame darker than the background, use the same color but less diluted.

On the opposite page are some ideas for creating striking frames. In the first example is a grid that imitates a support for climbing plants. In the second is a deep niche. In the third, a border is in relief with chiaroscuro. Add, of course, cutouts of flowers and leaves.

– Put the cutout in place, staggered with regards to the shading, and glue it on. Cut the whole design out from the cardboard.

– Glue the cutout onto the background (in this case made with marble-type paper), then trace the shading on the support and color it. To avoid the colors smudging, use a felt pen.

– Cover with glue, leave to dry, and apply a glossy finish.

RELIEF

This is a rather unusual technique to use for decoupage, but it allows you to obtain striking effects, particularly when the support being treated is uneven or badly damaged. You can, for example, revamp a flat surface with relief effects obtained from the outline of the cutout and create the illusion of inlaid, painted wood or of decorated stucco. Various ready-for-use products are on the market such as acrylic pumice, whether fine or rough (which is particularly strong); acrylic paste for modeling; and volume. Because of its weight, once dry, we advise the latter since it is suitable for all surfaces and can be easily worked with a painter's spatula. To make a relief, you need: an acetate sheet to trace the cutout and to create the templates (like those for the stencil), a craft knife, masking tape, a painter's spatula, a marker for glass and ceramics, fine-grained sandpaper, and volume. Naturally, after some practice you will be able to create more complex relief work or use just the spatula to make imaginatively smudged surfaces.

– Lay a sheet of acetate on the cutout and trace the outline with a marker.

– With a sharp craft knife, cut out the marked outline to make the template.

– Position the template on the support, securing it at one end with masking tape, and begin to evenly spread the volume with a spatula, creating a thickness of about $1/8$–$1/4$".

On the opposite page: decoupage on relief surfaces. In the first, a piece of lace cutout, glued and colored, creates an attractive effect. In the second, I applied colored photocopies of antique tiles to the relief. In the third, volume mixed with sea sand was spread like waves with a spatula.

– Delicately raise the template and leave to dry for a whole day until the relief is hard and dry.

– Sand the outlines and any other irregularities to achieve a smooth relief with fine-grained sandpaper.

– Apply the cutout, making it adhere to the outline. If it does not match the relief perfectly, glue its borders and turn in the excess part. Cover with glue and color. Trace the outlines in relief with a fine-tipped marker. Lightly smudge the cutout with the background color; it will then appear more integrated into the decoration.

FINISHING

Finishing employs all those final touches useful for protecting the decoration and the support; for giving a touch of brilliance; and, if desired, an antique look. Finishing touches are numerous and have different characteristics. Each one gives the finished project a different character; therefore, make it your practice not to use the same one all the time, but rather choose those most suitable for the work. The easiest to use is varnish with a water, oil, or alcohol base. Varnish creates a glossy, glazed, or opaque transparent film. Many coats have to be applied. I personally find that merely applying varnish over the decoration flattens the look of the work if it has not been previously treated with an effect technique. The varnish can also be combined with a crackling agent, which creates lovely effects, or it can be mixed with pigments. In any case, always choose nontoxic and ecological varnishes when possible.
Wax—whether neutral or mixed with oil colors, pigments, or metal-colored acrylics—creates a fascinating patina that is suitable for finishing furniture, walls, wood, and terracotta objects. It may also be applied to already-varnished surfaces and reapplied from time to time.
The final water-based varnish, glossy or opaque, is quite resistant as long as it is not washed with abrasive sponges. In the following example I used two different finishing touches on the same basic treatment. I decided on an acrylic background to which I applied the cutout, covered with glue, and aged with oil colors. Then, in the upper part I finished off with wax and in the lower part with aging varnish.

– Glue on the cutouts to an acrylic colored background. Leave to dry and cover the entire support with glue.

– Dab a cotton cloth in an oil color and spread it over the entire surface, including the cutouts. Make sure it penetrates into the grain of the wood. Leave to dry.

– Spread neutral wax with circular movements over the upper part and leave to dry.

On the opposite page: some examples of transparent finishing touches. Natural wood is on the top and wood painted with acrylic white is on the bottom. The same surfaces (from right to left) were treated with 1) a glossy varnish, 2) an oil-based varnish, 3) a water-based varnish, 4) an aging varnish, and lastly 5) an opaque oil varnish.
Above: wax finishings on wood colored with aniline dyes. Dark dyes are above and light dyes are below. The same surfaces were treated with wax mixed with gold acrylic and white pigment on the top row while only neutral wax was applied on the bottom row.

– Polish with a soft cloth. Spread more wax and polish again. To achieve a more glossy effect, apply some more polish; it will also make your work more resistant.

– Coat the lower part with various coats of aging varnish. The surface will take on a light amber color. If you wish, finish with wax.

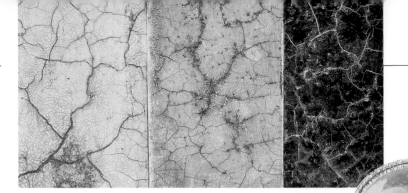

CRACKLING

Craquelé, a French word meaning "cracked", is a technique that imitates the cracks formed by time on some surfaces. I must say that it is perhaps the most difficult of the techniques described in this book because a satisfactory result depends on various factors. Most important of all is the background preparation on which to apply the aging varnish (oil varnish). The background must be smooth, absorbent, and perfectly isolated. If you have covered your decoupage with too much diluted glue or if the surface is uneven, it is likely that the oil will be absorbed and will not be able to interact with the water-based crackling varnish. The aging varnish must be spread evenly with a very soft brush or with a foam-rubber pad. The thickness of the coat is also most important: the thicker it is, the more evident the cracks will be. Furthermore, much attention must be given to its drying time. The aging varnish must still be sticky, like adhesive tape, before being covered with the crackling varnish. If the surface is too dry, cracks will not form, or they will be too small; if the surface is too damp, the crackling varnish will not adhere, forming drops. The chemical incompatibility between the two elements, the crackling varnish being water-based and the aging varnish being oil-based, is what creates the cracked effect. Even the drying time of the crackling varnish will influence the result. Usually a heat source like a heater, the sun, or the hot air of a hairdryer will help to heighten the effect. If you use a hairdryer, keep it away from the surface; otherwise, it could overheat and create air bubbles and flakes. The crackling varnish must also be spread evenly and thinly (better if with crisscrossing brush strokes). The climate and room temperature will also affect the end result. In short, you will never get the same effect on each object.

When the cracks have been formed and the surface has dried completely, you can highlight them with a pure oil color. For a softer effect, mix the color with neutral wax. Spread the color with a soft cloth using circular movements over the entire treated surface, pressing lightly. Then, with another clean cloth, remove any excess color. Allow to dry well and finish your work with a wax or an oil varnish. Never use a water-based varnish, as it will mix with the crackling varnish. Protect the crackled area with a strong finishing material, as it is very delicate.

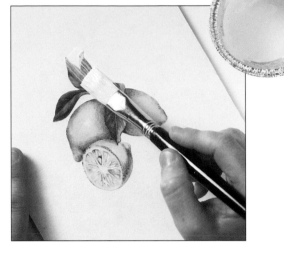

– Glue on the cutout. Let it dry and cover well with glue.

– Spread the aging varnish evenly with a soft brush. Leave to dry.

– When the surface of the aging varnish is not yet quite dry but is sticky like adhesive tape, brush on the crackling agent with crisscrossed brush strokes.

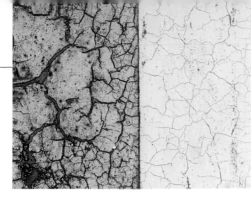

Various background tones and oil colors, which can also be combined, make it possible to obtain very different effects. On the opposite page are some examples. In the first square, both the aging and crackling varnishes have been thickly applied, thus creating bigger cracks. In the second, blue oil mixed with neutral wax was painted on a white background, creating a soft blue background. In the third example, I used a dark background to highlight the cracks that were previously painted with an oil color, the effect resembling marble. Above, in place of the aging varnish, I used regular oil varnish as a base for the crackling agent. In the first square the varnish was very sticky and I spread the crackling varnish on with a foam-rubber pad, the result being the formation of big, deep cracks. In the second square, the varnish was almost completely dry, creating small, unnoticeable cracks.

– With a hairdryer, heat the surface without going too near it. The first cracks will appear. Let it dry very well.

– With a soft cloth spread raw umber oil color over the entire crackled surface, pressing lightly and using circular movements.

– With a clean cloth remove any excess color and leave to dry. Finish off with a wax or an oil varnish.

WEAR-AND-TEAR EFFECT

Objects and furniture of a certain age acquire a look of wear and tear. To get this artificially, we have to partially remove and scrape away part of the paint until we see the bare surface or other underlying layers of colors. Other signs of aging are stains, haloes, and small holes. All of these signs are in the areas where the object has undergone most use, such as around door or drawer handles, the edges of a table, the seat of a chair, etc. Once the surface has been scraped and "ruined", it must be "dirtied" with pigmented wax or oil colors, and all the scratches must be filled in. Our cutout must also "feel" the passage of time and must, therefore, be treated to show wear and tear, especially around the outlines. To finish, use wax, which can be spread in several layers over a base of transparent varnish so as to make the treated surface more resistant.

– Spread a coat of acrylic chalk and then cover completely with a contrasting color. Leave to dry well.

– Sand the entire surface with medium-grained paper, concentrating on the corners and the outlines until you see the underlying color. If you wish to achieve a stronger effect, sand over once more with coarse-grained sandpaper.

– Glue on the cutout, cover it with glue, and let dry.

On the opposite page: examples of some colors that produce the wear-and-tear look: Left—a very thick coat of the color ochre was spread over the chalk background and scraped with coarse-grained sandpaper.
Center—a light blue acrylic was spread over a coat of chalk and then scraped and dirtied with a pearl gold acrylic.
Right—a copper acrylic was spread over a layer of dark green acrylic and then lightly scraped with coarse-grained sandpaper.

— With fine-grained sandpaper, lightly sand the outlines of the cutout.

— Brush over the project with a layer of aging varnish and leave to dry. Lastly, pass a soft cloth with some raw umber oil color or pigmented wax over certain parts of the object. Finish off with a wax or a transparent oil varnish.

PROJECTS

DESSERT BOWLS

Glass is easy to decorate with decoupage. If it is to be used for food, like these dessert and fruit cocktail bowls, it must be applied only on the outside. Choose brightly colored, natural motifs like fruit or flowers. They will help liven up your table and give it an original touch. Glass thus treated must be washed by hand in warm sudsy water with a nonabrasive sponge.

MATERIALS NEEDED:
- ACRYLIC COLORS
- WHITE GLUE (PVA)
- GLOSSY OIL VARNISH
- TURPENTINE
- ADHESIVE TAPE
- DOUBLE-SIDED
  ADHESIVE TAPE
- SMALL, FLAT BRUSHES
  (ONE SOFT ONE)
- MANICURE SCISSORS

– Position the cutouts on the outside of the bowl and secure them with double-sided adhesive tape.

– Glue on the cutouts one at a time. Leave to dry and then cover with glue.

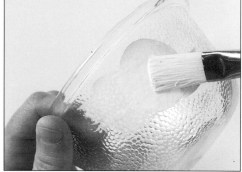

– Brush two even coats of acrylic on the cutouts and over the entire outside surface of the bowl. Leave to dry.

– Trace some irregular lines in yellow with a brush.

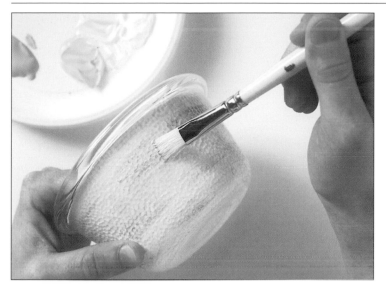

– Repeat the previous operation with the color green.

– Brush on a coat of transparent, glossy oil varnish and leave to dry. Apply more varnish at various times.

STORAGE BOX

This is an attractive idea for storing scarves, gloves, and other accessories at the end of the season. It can also be useful for holding letters, postcards, documents, or small objects. It is just a simple cardboard box decorated with travel motifs. You could even decorate it with fabric remnants or with motifs that will help you to identify immediately what is stored inside.

MATERIALS NEEDED:
- ACRYLIC COLORS
- NATURA SPONGE
- PLEXIGLAS TRIANGLE
- MASKING TAPE AND ADHESIVE TAPE
- WHITE GLUE (PVA)
- WATER-BASED FINISHING VARNISH
- ACETATE SHEET
- MARKER FOR GLASS AND CERAMICS
- MANICURE SCISSORS
- CRAFT KNIFE
- ASSORTED BRUSHES

– Mark the corners and the outside edges of the frame with masking tape. Cut out a rectangle of acetate and position it with the double-sided adhesive tape at the center of the box so that there is a space between the acetate sheet and the masking tape.

– Dip the sponge in the lightest color and dab the frame between the tape and the acetate. Leave to dry.

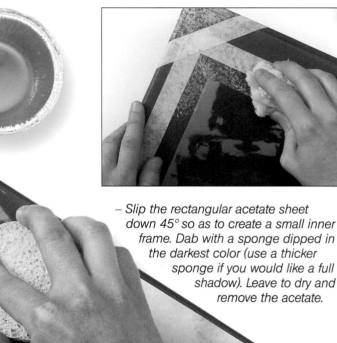

– Slip the rectangular acetate sheet down 45° so as to create a small inner frame. Dab with a sponge dipped in the darkest color (use a thicker sponge if you would like a full shadow). Leave to dry and remove the acetate.

– Glue on the cutouts and leave to dry. Cover the entire surface of the box with glue.

– Brush on several coats of a final water-based varnish.

NOTEBOOK WITH KITTENS

An old, somewhat damaged spiral ring binder was reinvented as this original notebook that is just right for your telephone numbers or photos.
The window cutouts look great glued onto a fake wall background, which was created using the technique with paint with glue.

MATERIALS NEEDED:
- WHITE WALL TEMPERA
- MULTIUSE STUCCO
- WHITE GLUE (PVA)
- SOFT SPONGE
- ACRYLIC COLOR
- MANICURE SCISSORS AND CRAFT KNIFE
- SOFT BRUSHES AND FLAT BRUSHES

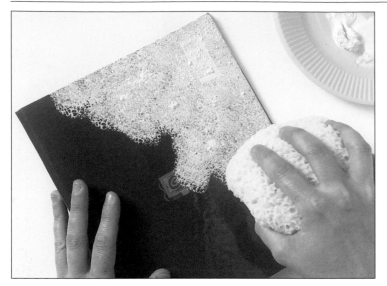

– *Prepare a paste with stucco, glue, and tempera and spread it fairly thickly by dabbing with the sponge. Leave to dry.*

– *Keep the brush flat. With just a little color on it, paint it over the treated surface, highlighting the relief. Leave to dry*

– Glue on the cutouts. When they are dry,
cover the entire surface with glue.

– Finish off with several coats of glue or, for
a glossy effect, with a water-based
final varnish.

TERRACOTTA VASE

There is an endless variety of decoration possibilities with which to turn an ordinary terracotta vase into an exclusive object for your home or garden. You could choose subjects which fit in with your surroundings by using the same fabrics or colors as your furnishings, or give reign to your imagination and create interesting contrasts. It would look original if you matched the decoration to the type of plant the vase is intended for, such as ethnic motifs for succulent plants, floral or gardening patterns for aromatic plants, and classical motifs for indoor plants. Terracotta is very porous, so remember to insulate it with acrylic chalk or with a few coats of glue before beginning to color the background.

MATERIALS NEEDED:
- OIL PENCILS
- TURPENTINE
- ACRYLIC CHALK
- SPRAY FIXATIVE SEALER
- OIL VARNISH
- NEUTRAL WAX
- RAW UMBER PIGMENT
- FINE STEEL WOOL
- COTTON CLOTHS
- MANICURE SCISSORS AND CRAFT KNIFE
- MARKERS

– Apply a coat of acrylic chalk to the outside of the vase and to the inner border. Leave to dry.

– Color the whole vase with the oil pencils, nuancing with various shades of blue.

– With a soft brush lightly dipped in turpentine, paint the colored surface until you obtain a well-blended background. Leave to dry.

– Spray on the fixative sealer (to avoid dirtying your hands with the oil pastels while you are gluing on the cutouts).

– Glue on the cutouts. When dry, pass glue over the entire surface.

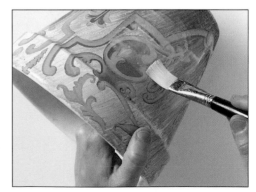

– Coat with oil varnish and leave to dry.

– Mix the neutral wax (2 parts) with the raw umber pigment (1 part) and spread it over the surface with fine steel wool.

– When the work is completely dry, spray on the fixative.

– Coat again with oil varnish.

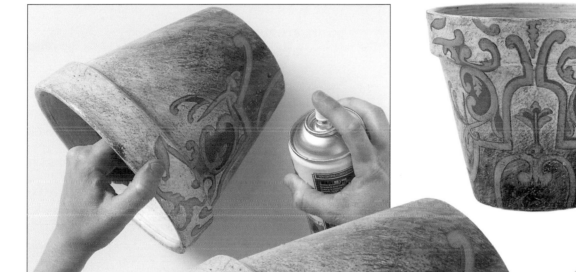

TOY CHEST

A natural wood box that is used to hold liquor bottles can be turned into a handy container for small objects such as those small games that tend to get strewn all over the house. The inside can be divided into compartments with wood or cardboard to house objects that are fragile or are part of a collection. As shown here, it can be colored in pastel shades with well-diluted acrylics (as a substitute for aniline dyes) and decorated with cute little bunnies.

MATERIALS NEEDED:
- ACRYLIC COLORS
- PLEXIGLAS TRIANGLE
- NEUTRAL WAX AND WHITE PIGMENT
- COTTON CLOTHS
- PENCIL
- MANICURE SCISSORS, CRAFT KNIFE, AND SCISSORS
- WHITE GLUE (PVA)
- FINAL WATER-BASED VARNISH
- BRUSHES OF VARIOUS SIZES
- SPATULA

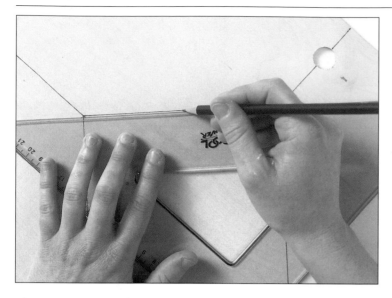

– Divide the lid into four sections and trace a square in the middle.

– Go over the pencil outline with the craft knife, scoring the wood to prevent the colors from mixing with each other.

– Dilute the acrylic color with a lot of water. Try spreading it on a concealed part of the box; the color must be transparent and show the veneer of the wood. When the right consistency has been obtained, color the various parts.

– Glue on the cutouts, leave to dry, and then cover with glue.

– Coat with a water-based varnish and leave to dry.

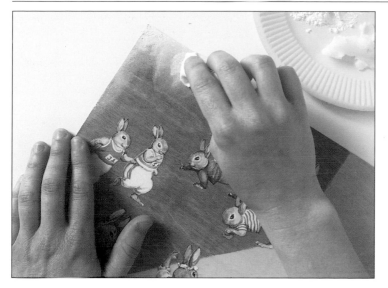

– Brush neutral wax mixed with white pigment over the corners and borders. Let dry and then polish.

– Spread the wax over the box without rubbing too much and leave to dry.

– Polish with a polishing cloth. Apply the wax once more and polish again. Repeat this operation several times.

ETHNIC TRAY

Trays with an ethnic motif, or with the same style as your dinnerware, can create a special atmosphere at the table.
You will need a rigid, shaped support (here ordinary plywood was used) and cutouts made of color photocopies from books and magazines. You could even use fabrics with exotic designs. They will be all the more attractive if aged with the wear-and-tear technique.

MATERIALS NEEDED:
- ACRYLIC COLORS
- WATER-BASED ENAMEL
- RAW UMBER OIL COLOR
- AGING VARNISH
- WHITE GLUE (PVA)
- FINE- AND COARSE-GRAINED SANDPAPER
- COTTON CLOTHS AND SOME BRUSHES

SHELL CHEST

This natural wood box is perfect for collecting shells. It was treated with water-based aniline dyes and decorated with a trompe-l'oeil effect to give depth to the lid and the cutouts. The shells could be substituted with cutouts of jewels, watches, or collector's items. Simple shading could then be drawn to give the impression that they are resting on the top. It is quite easy to do and the result is very unique.

MATERIALS NEEDED:
- WATER-BASED ANILINE DYES OF DIFFERENT SHADES
- SPRAY FIXATIVE SEALER
- AGING VARNISH
- PLEXIGLAS TRIANGLE
- MASKING TAPE
- BLACK PENCIL AND TRACING PENCIL
- DRAWING PAPER
- MANICURE SCISSORS, GLUE, FLAT BRUSH, AND SMALL BRUSHES

– Trace the outline of the lid on drawing paper. Draw a smaller rectangle for the frame. Position the cutouts and trace their contours.

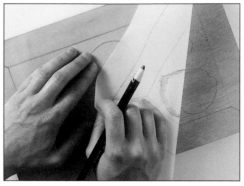

– Outline the back of the sheet with the tracing pencil and reproduce the project on the box.

– With the craft knife, score the outlines marked by the pencil.

– Prepare the water-based aniline dyes in different shades and color the frame, darker on top, lighter underneath, and the same color at the sides. Color the shadings of the cutouts with the darkest aniline dye. Leave to dry.

– Spray the fixative sealer to avoid staining the colors when spreading the glue.

– Position the cutouts with regards to the shadows.

– Glue on the cutouts and cover with glue.

– Coat several times with aging varnish. Leave to dry and, if desired, finish off with wax.

FRAME

Here is a different way to decorate a frame, which would make an attractive, original present. You could frame a mirror, a portrait, or one of your own drawings and decorate it with cutouts of abstract, geometric, or ethnic subjects. Applying a contrasting color unevenly over the relief will make it stand out. Remember that volume, the material used for the relief, needs a long drying time and that the project therefore takes some time to make.

MATERIALS NEEDED:
- ACRYLIC COLORS INCLUDING PEARL GOLD
- VOLUME
- DOUBLE-SIDED ADHESIVE TAPE
- WHITE GLUE (PVA) AND FINE-GRAINED SANDPAPER
- FINAL OIL VARNISH
- SHEET OF ACETATE
- MARKER FOR GLASS AND CERAMICS
- SPATULA
- CRAFT KNIFE AND BRUSHES
- CARDBOARD

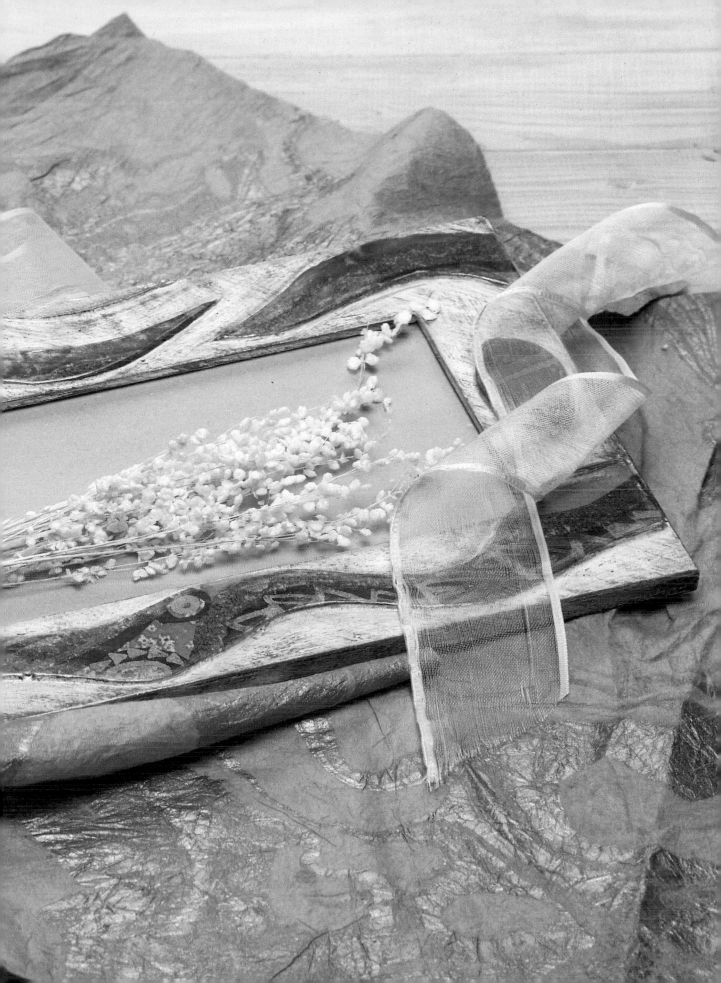

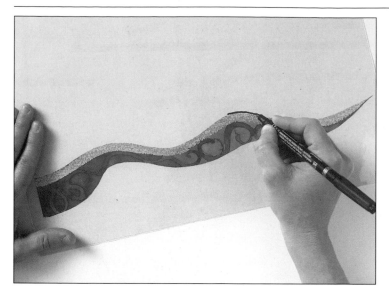

– Secure the cutout on a piece of cardboard with double-sided adhesive tape. Trace the outline on a sheet of acetate with the marker.

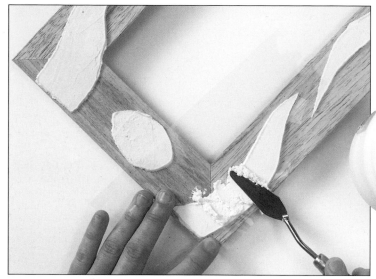

– Score the outline of the cutout with a craft knife and position the template on the frame, keeping it firm with masking tape. Cover with volume, spreading an even layer with the spatula.

– Raise the template immediately, making sure not to touch the relief with your fingers. Leave to dry thoroughly.

– Sand the surface and the borders of the relief with fine-grained sandpaper.

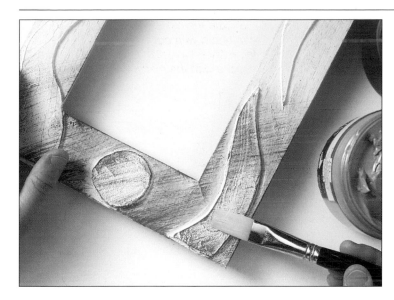

– Coat with white acrylic and leave to dry. Color the whole frame with irregular brushstrokes and several colors.

– Glue on the cutouts and cover with glue.

– Coat several times with oil varnish and leave to dry.

– With pearl gold acrylic, paint along the borders and outlines of the cutout.

COOKIE TIN

An ordinary tin, decorated with English style designs and treated with the crackling technique, can be quite charming. It can be used to serve cookies or biscuits with your tea or coffee. The choice of cutouts, the dabbed background, and the cracks all help give it an attractive, antique look.

MATERIALS NEEDED:
- ACRYLIC COLORS
- RAW UMBER OIL COLOR
- AGING AND CRACKLING VARNISHES
- FINAL OIL VARNISH
- TURPENTINE
- WHITE GLUE (PVA)
- CLEAN CLOTHS
- NATURAL SPONGE
- MANICURE SCISSORS AND CRAFT KNIFE
- SOFT BRUSHES

– Dab the box with the sponge, alternating between the acrylic colors ochre and sienna.

– Glue on the cutouts, leave to dry, and cover with glue.

– Coat evenly with aging varnish. Leave to dry until the varnish is slightly sticky.

– Coat evenly with cracking varnish, crisscrossing the brush strokes.

– Leave to dry. If you prefer to have more evident cracks, dry with a hairdryer, making sure to keep a distance from the surface.

– With a soft cloth, pass the raw umber oil color over the cracks, lightly pressing to make it penetrate. To obtain a softer effect, dilute with a little bit of wax. Remove any excess color with a clean cloth.

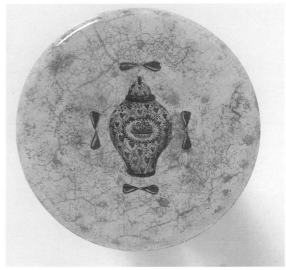

– Coat several times either with final oil varnish or aging varnish.

CRACKLED TRAY

Besides being useful, a tray can be a decorative element for the table or the kitchen. As the surface is flat and even, it can be decorated with all sorts of motifs. Attractive effects can be obtained by highlighting the shape with frames and borders. This tray, being quite large, can be used for serving dessert and has therefore been decorated with fresh motifs and bright colors suitable for all seasons.

MATERIALS NEEDED:
- ACRYLIC COLORS
- AGING AND CRACKLING VARNISHES
- RAW UMBER OIL COLOR
- CLEAN CLOTHS
- TURPENTINE
- WHITE GLUE (PVA) AND MANICURE SCISSORS
- ANILINE DYE (IF YOU WOULD LIKE TO FINISH OFF THE BACK OF THE TRAY WITH THE WOOD GRAIN VISIBLE)

– Dilute the orange acrylic color with a lot of water and pass it on the borders of the tray. Color the background with two shades of acrylic green.

– Glue strips of orange paper on the sides of the center rectangle.

– Position and glue on the cutouts. Leave to dry and cover with glue.

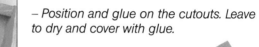

– Coat evenly with aging varnish.

– When the varnish is sticky, evenly apply the crackling varnish.

– Heat the surface with a hairdryer.

Pass the raw umber oil color over the cracks with a soft cloth. If you would like a softer effect, dilute the color with a little bit of turpentine.

– Remove any excess oil color with a clean cloth and coat several times either with final aging varnish or oil varnish.

WRAPPING-PAPER BIN

When you begin collecting lots of paper scraps for your decoupage hobby, you will need a handy container for putting them away in order. A steady umbrella-stand type in untreated wood is ideal because, thanks to its weight, it won't easily topple over. You can use your imagination on its spacious surfaces. I suggest a simple but highly effective technique such as paint with glue and a plain decoration for the bin: it will look colorful in its own right.

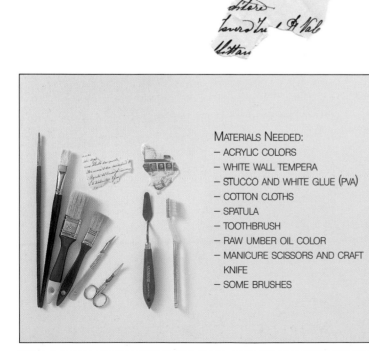

MATERIALS NEEDED:
- ACRYLIC COLORS
- WHITE WALL TEMPERA
- STUCCO AND WHITE GLUE (PVA)
- COTTON CLOTHS
- SPATULA
- TOOTHBRUSH
- RAW UMBER OIL COLOR
- MANICURE SCISSORS AND CRAFT KNIFE
- SOME BRUSHES

– Prepare the paste with glue, stucco, and wall tempera.

– Spread it rather thickly with crisscrossed brush strokes using a toothbrush. Leave to dry.

– Dip the brush in a little bit of color and pass it flat (not pointed) over the stucco relief. Overlap various colors.

– Glue on the cutouts (some could also be torn), leave to dry, and cover with glue.

– Coat with final oil varnish and leave to dry.

– With raw umber oil color, smudge the surfaces unevenly without pressing so that you apply the color only on the relief.

– Remove any excess color and coat several times with either final oil varnish or neutral wax.

TEA CADDY

This raw wood jar has been treated to recall old stoneware crockery. The crackling technique was used to obtain very small cracks. The motifs are black and white photocopies of old sample designs. As this jar is being used as a caddy for tea bags, it has not been treated inside.

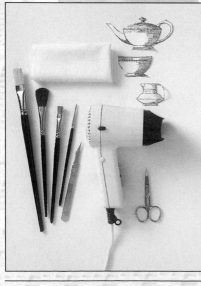

MATERIALS NEEDED:
- WHITE ACRYLIC COLOR
- AGING AND CRACKLING VARNISHES
- FINAL OIL VARNISH
- BLACK OR RAW UMBER OIL COLOR
- TURPENTINE AND WHITE GLUE (PVA)
- HAIRDRYER
- CLEAN CLOTHS
- MANICURE SCISSORS, CRAFT KNIFE, AND SOFT BRUSHES (SOME SMALL ONES)

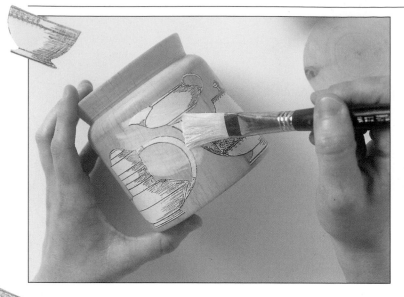

– Glue the cutouts onto the natural wood background of the jar. Leave to dry and then cover with glue.

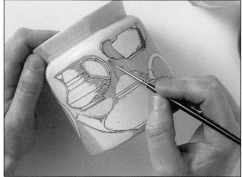

– With a small brush, fill all the empty spaces with white acrylic, leaving a colorless border around the outlines of the cutouts. Leave to dry.

– Coat evenly with aging varnish.

– When this varnish is almost dry (sticky), apply a light coat of crackling varnish. Leave to dry at room temperature.

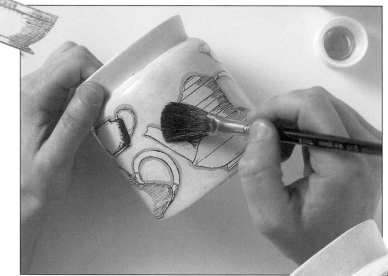

– Lightly press the oil color in the cracks.
If you use black oil color, the result will
be more drastic: if you prefer a softer look,
use raw umber oil color. Remove any
excess color.

– Coat several
times with final oil
varnish.

SOME
SUGGESTIONS

TRAYS

If you are tackling decoupage for the first time, a tray is perfect to begin with. Trays are available in all shapes and sizes, such as wood, plastic, metal, and mixed compounds. They can be treated with aniline dyes to add value to the wood or colored with acrylic colors using almost any of the techniques illustrated in the beginning of this book. At the top of the opposite page is a small wicker tray that has been decorated only along the borders with a blue and white mosaic motif. It was then protected with glazed oil varnish. The tray on which it is resting has wicker borders and a plywood base, which is decorated with ticket, postcard, brochure, and map cutouts. It was treated with crackling varnish and protected with a oil varnish and wax. The tray with the orange borders was made as shown on pages 90 to 93. The shape of the tray in the foreground was decorated with an American 1950's theme. The bottom is blue (a lighter shade than the borders) and has been highlighted by an ivory frame. Cake cutouts rest on fake shadows.

Here are two completely different trays to show the numerous decorating possibilities offered by this technique. The oval, ethnic-type tray was painted with glossy black enamel. Recycled paper was then applied to the base, bordered by twine. The motifs on the border, cut with a colored margin to make them stand out, are the same. The work was protected with a glossy oil varnish.

The rectangular tray was instead aged with the wear-and-tear technique. First treated with aniline dyes, it was then evenly scratched. The cutouts were painted over with burnt umber oil color. After a coating of aging varnish, several layers of wax were applied.

FRAMES

Frames are another type of support suitable for creating original objects. The decoration can be chosen to highlight the subject to be framed. On the top of the opposite page, green acrylic was spread on the background. Photocopies of old lock designs were glued on and the ornaments were painted in acrylic gold. The frame underneath was made with photocopies of fabrics and protected with aging varnish and pigmented wax.

On this page is a frame that used the paint-with-wax technique for the background. The cutouts were highlighted by using various colors. They were then slightly sanded around the outlines and placed over the frame's border and base. Underneath is the frame in relief as illustrated on pages 82–85.

LETTER RACK

Shown here is a useful letter rack for holding correspondence and notes. It was decorated with old-time sailing boats, recalling typical nautical furnishing. The curving lines of the wood, treated with an old walnut aniline dye, were glued with strips of paper designs of nautical ropes. The work was then protected with glossy oil varnish and wax.

BOXES

Shoe boxes, food containers, gift boxes, and the like can easily be recycled into containers for all tastes and all ages. They can be used instead of the usual wrapping paper for all occasions. Specialized shops offer boxes of all shapes and sizes that are untreated or covered with canvas or special paper, which can act as backgrounds. Such, for example, is the case with the box shown on the opposite page; it was covered in rice paper, decorated with children's motifs, and then finished with a final water-based varnish. Below is the box with shells illustrated on pages 78–81. Another wooden box is decorated with

cutouts of old currency. In the foreground below are two small wooden boxes for holding jewelry with English-style decorations. On the left is an original candy box with African designs. Lastly, a cardboard pencil box for children is decorated with attractive animal motifs.

TOY CHEST

This useful and attractive chest for games was made from an ordinary wooden box for wine bottles.

The background was painted in green acrylic. The cutouts were taken from gift-wrapping paper and photocopies of old cards and children's books. A personal touch was then written with an acrylic color on the lid. The work is protected with several coats of a final water-based varnish.

Stuffed fabric lines the inside and the outer borders. Two brass handles were screwed on at the sides.

Lastly, a strong piece of cotton tape was secured under the lid to help open and close the chest.

FLOWER POTS

A good way
to make use
of old, chipped, or damaged terracotta
vases is to decorate them attractively and
make flowers pots out of them. Several
coatings of glue or acrylic plaster are
essential to insulate the terracotta, which
is very absorbent, before treating it. The
blue and white mosaic on the pot above
was made on a base of smudged light
blue-colored chalk. I invented the cutouts.
Crackle varnish was used to finish.
Glazed oil varnish and wax were used to
protect the vase. The red and blue pot
was made with oil
pencils and
finished with a
glossy oil varnish.
The light-colored
pot was sponge-
treated with the
paint-with-glue
technique and colored
with acrylics. The
border decoration was
done with a marker.

PLACE MATS

Place mats are an excellent way to set a table quickly and lightheartedly. Decoration possibilities are endless and you can match the style of your kitchen and dinnerware, or you can just create something completely different.

In the big photo below, a piece of plywood was completely covered with old labels. A frame of tissue paper was laid over the borders and the underlying designs to show through. The work was finished off with final oil varnish pigmented with raw umber oil color.

The background of the place mat on the adjoining page was made with wrapping paper of two different colors over which fruit cutouts were glued. The decoration was then treated with the wear-and-tear technique and protected with a final oil varnish.

SCHOOL DESK

This desk required a great deal of effort to clean and treat. Found at a flea market, it was completely covered by a layer of formica that had to be patiently stripped and sandpapered. The top was insulated with acrylic chalk and coated many times with a light blue acrylic color. The cutouts were glued on and the whole top was treated with the wear-and-tear technique. It was then protected with several coats of a final water-based varnish. The wooden structure was colored with an old walnut aniline dye and protected with two coats of a final oil varnish and wax.

IRGENDWO NOTGELANDET,
29. JANUAR
MEINE ALLERLIEBSTE SOPHIE,
DU MACHST DIR BESTIMMT SORGEN, MUßT DU ABER
NICHT. DER BALLONFLUG WAR EINFACH KLASSE. AUCH
WENN DAS MIT DER SCHNUR NICHT SO
GEPLANT WAR ALS DU IMMER
KLEINER WURDEST, HATTE ICH DOCH EIN
BIßCHEN ANGST. UND SO RICHTIG ANGST
BEKAM ICH, ALS DIESE KIRCHTURMUHR
MIT IHREN SPITZEN ZEIGERN DEN BALLONS
SO NAHE KAM. STELL DIR MAL VOR, WENN
DA HINEINGEPIEKST HATTEN! ZUM GLÜCK BRACHTE MICH
EINE WINDBÖE IN SICHERHEIT. STEUERN KANN MAN
DIE
FELIX.

PAPIER-MÂCHÉ BOWLS

These bowls, which look as if made of terracotta or wood, have actually been made with papier-mâché and decorated with decoupage. Thanks to this beautiful material the final effect is surprising. The bases were treated with acrylic colors and smudged with contrasting shades, particularly on the borders (to imitate aging). The cutouts were also faded and smudged. For protection, a coat of final water-based varnish was applied first and then with wax pigmented with raw umber and natural ochre. These bowls can be used as containers for succulent plant combinations or for dried fruit, spices, or small objects.

MOCK BOOKS

Small-sized boxes with a drawer or book-style openings, where you could keep personal objects, can simulate books that can be inserted among real books in a bookcase or on a bookshelf. Decorate the back and cover with imitations of old titles or photocopy books that you already have. Color the borders with an ivory acrylic color to make them look like pages. Heavy wooden boards can also be decorated and used as bookends.

NOTEBOOKS

Old notebooks or spiral binders can be decorated and reused as books for photos, recipes, and travel diaries. Choose cutouts suitable to the theme or let your imagination run wild. Use prints taken from newspapers, fabrics, or photocopies of family photos. Above on the opposite page is a notebook for gardening made with English paper. Below, for those who gamble, is an index book treated with aging varnish and covered with subjects from the ancient Cabala. On the right of this page is the notebook with kittens illustrated on pages 62–65. Below is a recipe book with appropriate cutouts glued on a sponged background and protected with a water-based varnish.

FOR KIDS

A cardboard display case from a perfume department store was used to make these shelves. The untreated cardboard background was colored in pastel shades while the shelves were kept in their original color. Cutouts from English paper with charming little bears were applied to the background and then protected with a final water-based varnish. These shelves, at the same time robust and light, represent a useful and safe object in which games or small books can be stored away. It would function equally well if hung on a wall or stood on a desk.

KEY HANGER

The glass was removed from an octagonal frame to turn it into this very useful key hanger, which can be hung in the hallway or in the garage.

The base was colored in light blue and sea green acrylics. It was aged and smudged with white-pigmented wax. The cutouts are reproductions of ancient locks and handles. Several coatings of neutral wax protect the whole object. The hooks were glued on and then screwed on from the back of the object to hold the weight of the keys.

131

FURNISHING
WITH DECOUPAGE

As we have seen, decoupage can be applied to all sorts of surfaces and offers numerous possibilities in choosing a project. Furnishing with this technique means that you are not limited to decorating small objects or pieces of furniture, but you are able to create a unique, personal style in your own house. Around the middle of the 18th century, and for over a hundred years later, it was common in England to apply cutouts from books, prints, and friezes to walls. These walls were brightly colored to highlight the glued decorations. Today, thanks to the numerous reproduction possibilities that are available (from books, photocopies, magazines, etc.), we have an endless variety of subjects to choose for our walls. We need only to prepare a project that fits in with our existing furnishings. For example, a child's room could be brightened by decorating all of the furniture with matching cutouts.
In other rooms you could create mock frames, borders, or trompe l'oeil effects. In the bathroom and kitchen, tiles and glazed walls can be decorated to hide the defects of worn doors and window frames.

PRINT ROOM

The technique for creating decorated walls is very simple. Color the wall as desired, prepare a precise project, cut out your subjects, and glue them on as shown on the opening pages of this book. When they are dry, cover them with glue. To prevent the glue from dripping and creating unsightly drops, dilute it with a little bit of water and spread it from the bottom upward on the cutouts. Protect your work with several coats of a final water-based varnish, preferably opaque. If the wall is often touched, the protection must be stronger; so, brush over the wall with some final oil varnish. To achieve a very elegant effect, apply neutral wax in several coats.

Fig. 654.

Fig. 657.

Fig. 662.

Fig. 663.

An old English print depicting shells was glued on a wall colored with orange tempera to set off the shadings of the drawings. A slight blue and ivory perspective on the inner sides of the frame creates a pleasant, deep effect, which is suitable for the kitchen or bathroom.

Here the background wall was colored with the sponging technique to recall the irregular look of stone. The cutout is an enlarged photocopy taken from a book to which a transparent shadow has been added (with diluted acrylic) directly onto the wall to give the impression of relief. The same was done on the lower border. The work was then protected with an opaque final water-based varnish.

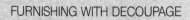

This frieze, photocopied from a book, was colored with watercolors and glued to a plastered wall. The lines that enclose the border underneath were done with acrylic paint. This type of stucco-like cutout is suitable for decorating high ceilings and walls.

1. 2. Amphora. 3. Hydria. 4. Kanne. 5. Hydria. 6. Amphora. 7. Le[
[Sämtlich aus dem Museum zu Berlin.

Printed in Italy by Grafiche Tassotti. N° 156

This print is a classical design of ancient Greek urns which has been glued to a wall colored in yellow-ochre tempera. The frame was obtained by color photocopying from a book illustrating carpets and old tapestries. The work was protected with final oil varnish and wax. It would look great as a decoration for a collector's study.

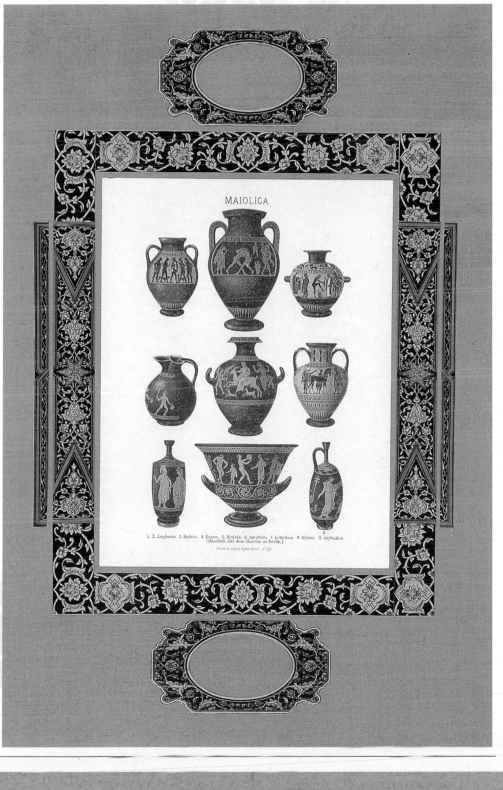

MAIOLICA

1. 2. Amphora. 3. Hydria. 4. Kanne. 5. Hydria. 6. Amphora. 7. Lekytlos. 8. Krater. 9. Aryballos.
[Sämmtlich aus dem Museum zu Berlin.]

6

9

s. 8. Krater. 9. Aryballo

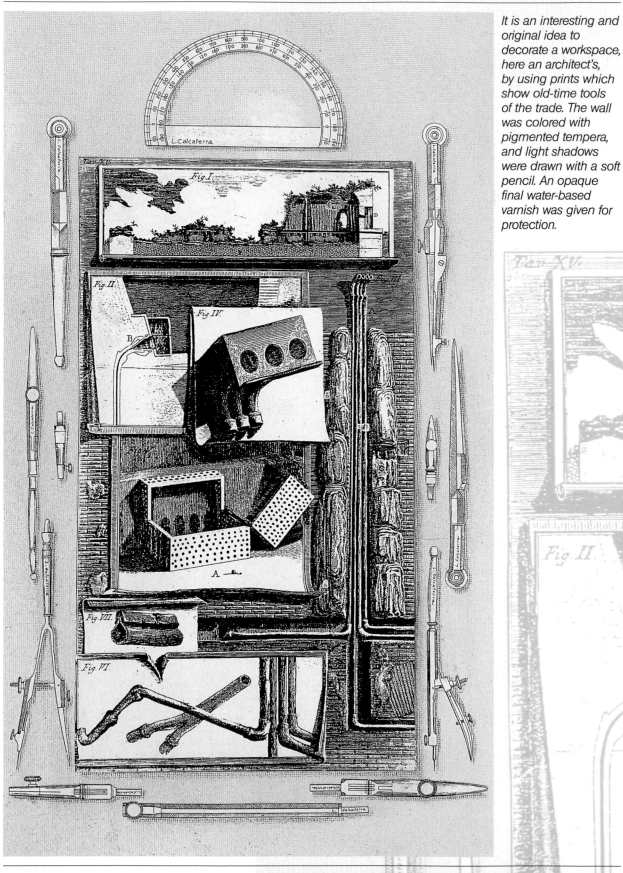

It is an interesting and original idea to decorate a workspace, here an architect's, by using prints which show old-time tools of the trade. The wall was colored with pigmented tempera, and light shadows were drawn with a soft pencil. An opaque final water-based varnish was given for protection.

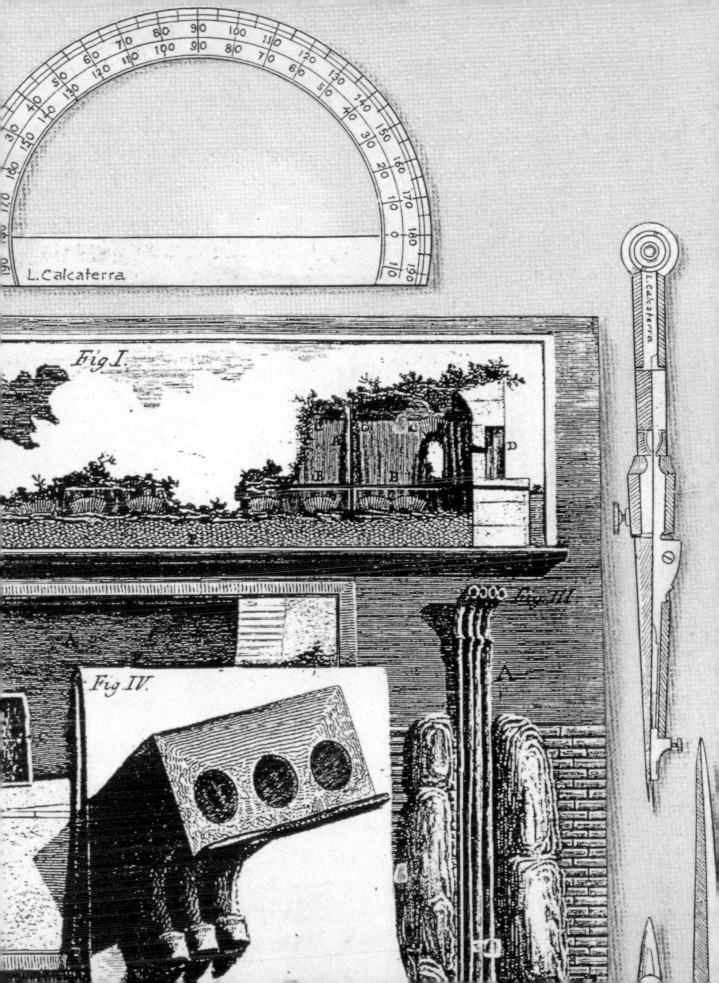

L. Calcaterra

Fig I.

Fig IV.

L. Calcaterra

FURNISHING WITH DECOUPAGE

Here are some suggestions for creating frames and borders in different environments. On the top of this page are photocopies taken from an old manual for artists and used to create a border suitable for a study. The contrast between the background and the cutouts is accentuated by the pencil-drawn shadows. In the center is an idea for a children's room. The patchwork effect of the cutouts is softened by the light blue background with pastel lines. Below are shells, stones, and dried leaves on an ivory and dusty rose background created for a room especially dedicated to relaxing.

Above are bright colors for the cutouts that were glued on a smudged orange and red background and then framed by lines hand-traced with oil pencils. This is perfect for brightening a hallway or a dark corner. In the center can be seen a graphic frame, which plays on contrasts, and would look great in bathrooms, kitchens, and modern settings. Below is some ethnic embroidery for your home.

TILES

The market offers splendid reproductions of antique tiles with motifs copied from the traditions of Italian majolica, Islamic, medieval, Oriental, and other various cultures. These tiles create a uniquely fascinating environment, but they are, unfortunately, too expensive to buy. Decoupage offers an excellent imitation technique, which enables you to choose your own subjects. The gluing technique for the cutouts is described at the beginning of this book. Furthermore, as tiles are smooth, an aging effect can be obtained with the crackling or wear-and-tear techniques. The decoration must be well protected as it is often applied in damp places such as bathrooms and kitchens. Very resistant glazing products are available on the market (such as those for finishing floors and parquet). Instead of buying these products, you can coat the tiles with several layers of a final water-based or oil-based varnish. Remember that tiles treated this way tend to go slightly yellow over the years and that they have to be washed with nonabrasive sponges and detergents. As a further suggestion, your decoration could be applied to wood panels and secured to the walls wherever you like, creating unusual embellishments that can be easily removed when desired.

A classical decoration in white and blue that is suitable for both the kitchen and the bathroom. Repetition of the motif creates a harmonious, restrained effect. Applied to a panel, it can frame mirrors and small niches. These tiles recall the mid-19th-century and early-20th-century periods. The famous Portuguese azulejos are particularly splendid.

Here is an attractive pot stand for everyday use. The tile was decorated, glued to a plywood panel, and framed with strips that match the cutouts. The motif could be used for walls or other accessories. Heat-resistant varnishes were used for final protection.

Below is a composition suitable for the kitchen. It was obtained from color photocopies of antique 17th-century tiles. The enlarged cutout was calculated in proportion to the support to be decorated. Several coats of a glazed final water-based varnish were applied for protection. The background wall was colored with a water-based enamel paint. The same results are also easily obtained with photocopies of Islamic tiles or Italian majolica.

Illustrations from an old botany book form the subject of these very original tiles. They are suitable for various types of use, whether in the kitchen or in a study. They can be combined with plain-colored tiles or can be used to create a running frieze. Aging with the crackling technique obviously requires more time and patience but results in striking effects. Strong protection is needed; therefore, it is best to use a glazing product or apply various coats of a glossy final oil varnish. The choice of subject is up to you, so enjoy trying shells, fish, butterflies, and other motifs taken from old books.

Here are some ethnic motifs for borders. The decoration must naturally match the color of the walls (in this case they were sponged in warm tones) and the surrounding furnishings. Endless suggestions can be picked from books and magazines that illustrate the traditional art of people and cultures around the world. Travel buffs can create unique borders that recreate memories from their journeys.

As shown below, a simple frame of tiles attached to the wall or on panels can make your kitchen or dining room appear more welcoming. In this project, cutouts from English papers were used with designs that evoke feelings of leisure and relaxation. Many designs can be found that have gardening instruments and equipment, which are suitable for verandas or porches.

Another idea is that of creating richly decorated tiles that can be placed in strategic corners or places in your home. You can play around not only with the patterns but also with the size of the tiles, which range from small to large. The choice of design is practically endless. In the two tiles shown here, the hen cutouts have been glued to small pieces aged with raw umber oil colors and then protected with a final oil varnish and wax.

This frame, which reproduces tableware, has been subjected to the aging technique. The dark patina that gives a used look has been obtained with two coats of an aging varnish, while the soiled edges are the result of various levels of raw umber natural oil color. It is very suitable for the kitchen and could be applied to a panel to frame a kitchen dresser or plate rack. Designs can be taken from catalogues, magazines, and books that deal with china and ceramics. You could even reproduce designs from old family pieces of tableware—photocopy them and then apply to the tiles.

DOORS AND WINDOWS

It is very easy to apply decoupage to door and window frames, and besides being a very decorative effect, helps to hide small defects caused by time and normal wear and tear.
It also highlights the colors and motifs of doors, hallways, and windows. The technique for gluing is described at the beginning of this book. As protection, you could use a final water-based varnish that does not turn yellow. Ornaments or borders made with a brush or stencil could also be added to the cutouts to show off your work.
This square window overlooks a small balcony. It illuminates the study. The owners' enthusiasm for gardening and botany, added to the need to brighten up a rather dark area, led to the choice of this English paper that reproduces stylized but lively pots and plants.

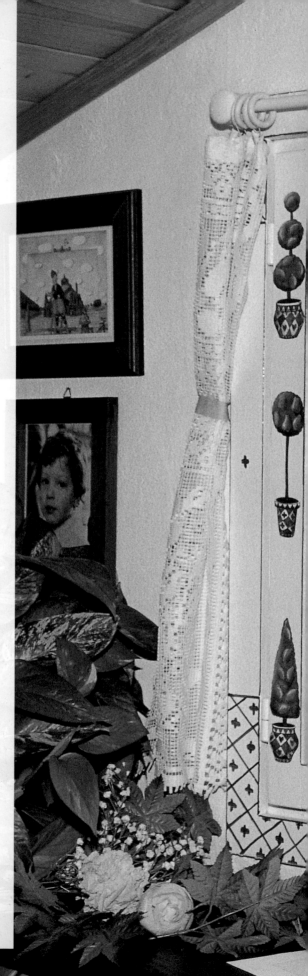

Before gluing on the cutouts, the inner frame around the panes was colored with yellow to highlight the strong effect made by the blue in the pots.

With a brush, blue rhombs were irregularly drawn on the window frames. The cutouts were protected with a glossy final water-based varnish.

A TOUCH OF MEXICO

There is a touch of Mexico in this little window that overlooks an inner courtyard. The courtyard needed a decoration which would draw attention from the rather unattractive building across from it. The building's yellow color meant that warm, sunny colors were needed.

To emphasize the warm atmosphere, a thick yellow frame was created around the old window frame and painted with white water-based enamel paint.

The paper reproduces richly colored geometrical motifs and it was deliberately cut unevenly in border strips. This was a little trick to hide the various

irregularities of the worn window frame. The cutouts were then protected with a glazed final water-based varnish.

This room is furnished with period furniture mixed with modern in warm, colors. The presence of a terrace, as well as numerous indoor plants, called for a decoration that would create continuity between the two environments. The two panels on the French window were therefore colored a pastel shade of green using the sponging method. Paper, with floral motifs on a light yellow background, was glued to the panels. The design is classical, but it matches the modern red armchair and the curtain.

The background panels were colored in light green. Some yellow was added in for the first sponging and white in the second. The sponge is an imitation natural sea sponge and is round in shape. When the color was dry, the cutouts were glued on and a frame was formed. Once dry, the cutouts were covered with glue. Dark red lines were traced with a brush to underemphasize the cutouts and the light green around the pane frames. Several coats of a glazed final water-based varnish were applied for protection.

INDEX